Bret and His Pet

Kelly Doudna

Consulting Editor, Diane Craig, M.A./Reading Specialist

Published by ABDO Publishing Company, 4940 Viking Drive, Edina, Minnesota 55435.

Printed in the United States.

Credits
Edited by: Pam Price
Curriculum Coordinator: Nancy Tuminelly
Cover and Interior Design and Production: Mighty Media
Photo Credits: AbleStock, Brand X Pictures, Comstock, Photodisc

Library of Congress Cataloging-in-Publication Data

Doudna, Kelly, 1963-
    Bret and his pet / Kelly Doudna.
        p. cm. -- (First rhymes)
    ISBN 1-59679-489-5 (hardcover)
    ISBN 1-59679-490-9 (paperback)
        1. English language--Rhyme--Juvenile literature. I. Title. II. Series.

PE1517.D625 2006
808.1--dc22

                                                                                    2005048047

SandCastle™ books are created by a professional team of educators, reading specialists, and content developers around five essential components that include phonemic awareness, phonics, vocabulary, text comprehension, and fluency. All books are written, reviewed, and leveled for guided reading and early intervention reading, and designed for use in shared, guided, and independent reading and writing activities to support a balanced approach to literacy instruction.

Let Us Know

After reading the book, SandCastle would like you to tell us your stories about reading. What is your favorite page? Was there something hard that you needed help with? Share the ups and downs of learning to read. We want to hear from you! To get posted on the ABDO Publishing Company Web site, send us e-mail at:

sandcastle@abdopub.com

SandCastle Level: Beginning

-et

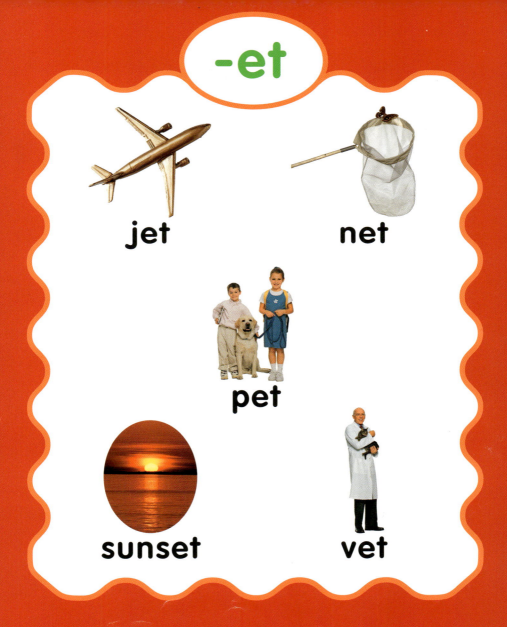

jet

net

pet

sunset

vet

Look at the .

See the  .

Here is a  .

Look at the .

He is a  .

The jet can fly.

The net is white.

This pet is a dog.

The sunset is pretty.

The vet is nice.

Bret and His Pet

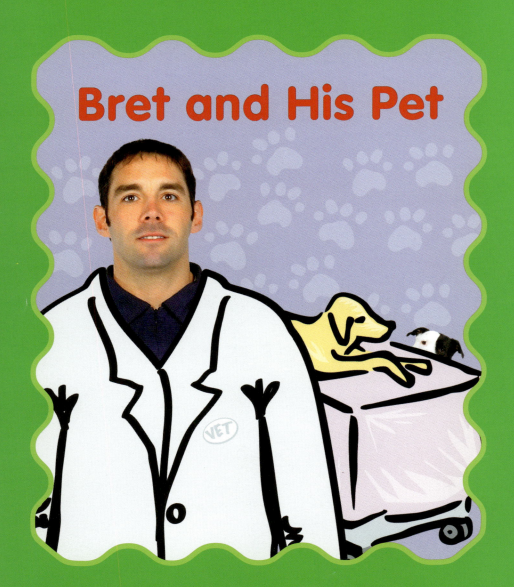

Bret is a vet.

16

Bret the vet
has a pet.

18

Bret the vet
wants to take his pet
on a big jet.

Bret the vet
needs a net
to catch his pet
and get him on the jet.

After Bret the vet
gets his pet
in the net
and on the jet,
they fly into the sunset.

About SandCastle™

A professional team of educators, reading specialists, and content developers created the SandCastle™ series to support young readers as they develop reading skills and strategies and increase their general knowledge. The SandCastle™ series has four levels that correspond to early literacy development in young children. The levels are provided to help teachers and parents select the appropriate books for young readers.

Emerging Readers
(no flags)

Beginning Readers
(1 flag)

Transitional Readers
(2 flags)

Fluent Readers
(3 flags)

These levels are meant only as a guide. All levels are subject to change.

To see a complete list of SandCastle™ books and other nonfiction titles from ABDO Publishing Company, visit **www.abdopub.com** or contact us at:
4940 Viking Drive, Edina, Minnesota 55435 • 1-800-800-1312 • fax: 1-952-831-1632